Occupied

Carol Mirakove

THE FRANCES JAFFER BOOK AWARD

KELSEY ST. PRESS

This award for the publication of a first book honors the memory of Bay Area poet, editor and feminist Frances Jaffer, 1921–1999.

Judge: Mei-mei Berssenbrugge

Library of Congress Cataloging-in-Publication Data

Mirakove, Carol.
  Occupied / Carol Mirakove.
      p. cm.
  Includes bibliographical references.
  ISBN 0-932716-66-0 (pbk. : alk. paper)
1. Afghanistan—History—2001—Poetry.   2. Iraq War, 2003—Literature and the war.
3. American poetry—21st century.   4. Protest poetry, American.   I. Title.
  PS3563.I683O28 2004
  811'.6—dc22

                                    2004005030

Series design by Poulson/Gluck Design

Text is set in 10 point Optima.
Printed in an edition of 600.

All orders to: Small Press Distribution
                  800-869-7553   email: orders@spdbooks.org

Please note: We do not read unsolicited manuscripts for this award.

You can visit Kelsey St. Press online at: www.kelseyst.com

CONTENTS

AFGHANISTAN

IRAQ

NEW ORDER

these poems are dedicated to

Amy Goodman

Arundhati Roy

and the memory of
Paul Wellstone
(1944–2002)

Occupied

AFGHANISTAN

I beg them

imagine
your neighbor
a woman in her 50s
screaming in agony
wounded by a bomb

                    PHILIP M. CONDIT

your neighbor

                    NICHOLAS D. CHABRAJA

and you wait
for aid

                    RONALD SUGAR

you wait

                    VANCE D. COFFMAN

the woman is actual
but distant
she's a character
in a dream
that is my life
I appear to her
standing behind
the men I cannot kill

3rd grade on the 3rd world

10/7/2001: Kabul renamed the front-line district

      parents plant text & photos by a seed I would
succumb. not surprised by destruction I bought
                       a guide-kitten awed & I
         have found the people, can
    observe what I am
doing. blasting out
     they finger the blue & double
     as homes — "a third of the city
           is rubble."

where are the sandboxes in this picture?

"Don't believe what the grown-ups are saying....Don't ever believe what
Osama bin Laden told you about America....We promise after the war is over
we will never hurt your country again." — Stewart[*]

"Be careful! The whole world is about to attack you, and so is America!"
— Victor

          "they"
"point to my bulging   pocket"
          everyone a gun "with the safety catch
    on"   the razor wire
                         duckling cuts
                         youthful

[*]Attributed quotes come from letters sent by Mrs. Sugar's 3rd-grade class in Fort Worth,
Texas, to their counterparts in Afghanistan. Other quoted phrases were found or compiled
from various texts on Afghanistan.

sandbags I am still
learning ((the other))
& filthy

"In America,
it is not evil. If it was, I wouldn't
be here. Sincerely, Martin"

"it"   "bucks" "I" —
"We are shooting the campsites at night
so you don't get hurt."

December 2002: land mines kill 20–25 Afghans each day

pulling me away by my collar
my guide
I take the opportunity
& garner a mental ward,
familiar with the markings:
my mouth — my heart —
para / graphing
hospitals I felt an overwhelming
biography — concocted
tale & a reason ("No, no, we just" —)
are buying "What is Islam?" on CD at the bodega &
in public are we jockeyed
to be photoed?

you are going to love it here

4

Victor: "Don't believe what Osama bin Laden told you about America."

Breanna: "[In America] you can believe anything you want to believe."

K. RUPERT MURDOCH

:: checkpoint ::

fed up an airticket

ricocheted

we drive straight through

hoping to avoid

"9/11" & succeeding   AHMAD SHAH MASSOUD

the world we make

worth "communicated" saving

I can't list any more children

"through a grill"   "in the fence"

"with their relatives"

"on the inside."

& of parentage: stumbling upon

PAUL WOLFOWITZ

special services & not

setting them on fire

to safety   *in one tiny room*

"relating"   *I spotted*

"unimaginable"   *children, who looked to be*

"deeds"   *the age of twelve*

like a cat nap.   *locked up.*

women & children

convivance   peels the pillow off the suffocating cagebird & widespread:
she washes your hair in a secular lather, mobile streams. puppets for play &
treason drained of meaning. populace policies. packed spring water.

tempest MEENA, 31 — killed at the barrels of KHAD. Afghan girls sold for
wheat and brides. pressed collectibles, still may suffer.

staggering seeds the apprehension, rising rags to altar breasts. bedrock cele-
brates the stories of our curves & our soft stomachs. evoking spirits — parents
— sending kids to bed all tucked in blankees & cradling dreams. burning the
burqa, teaching & practicing   medicine & law

+

pebble game   —   goes first & picks up   —   hopscotch
kabadi   —   crosses line & goes between   —   running bases
eagle   —   stands watch & runs to catch   —   manhunt
kite-flying   —   runs sand & meets with   —   kite-flying

+

leaving purpose. apprentice spinning. sleep wizard, magic lamps, lullaby
refrain & dog-ears the page.

faulty intelligence

a USAmerican plane bombards
Kakrak on July 1, suspecting Taliban,
discovering a slaughtered
engagement party[*]

President BUSH called
President HAMID KARZAI
of Afghanistan   *picking up limbs*
on Friday   *from streets & an orchard*
to express   *carrying the wounded*
his sympathy   *to the mosque*

                             they had been
                             enjoying the night air
USAmerican soldiers   *and singing*
visibly shocked   *wedding songs at 1am*
and saddened   *drinking tea & chatting*

killed 48   *sleeping boys on a rooftop*
injured 117   *hands of the women*
civilian   *what's done cannot be*
shrapnel   *undone*

"the greatest effect was on the house next door"

scarlet flowers still bloom

[*]as reported by Carlotta Gall in *The New York Times*, July 8, 2002

7

congealed blood   *tugging her veil*
under an arch   *across her face*
wept in a corner   *"write about this"*
wept over bloody clothes *make them leave us*

"my grandson's and my daughter's mouths
were full of dust"

DICK CHENEY

SALAM PAX
thinks we have forgotten
Afghanistan

I don't know the difference
between my skirt and this table

JAMES A. BAKER III
but I have not forgotten

we have not forgotten

GEORGE W. BUSH

IRAQ

I remember

counterpoint & me too

NORTH KOREA
FCC
VENEZUELA

Chile, deadened to apathy by two decades of dictatorship. AUGUSTO PINOCHET. what will happen to us. has happened. is. active.

+

I remember lies in 1964, when then-president LYNDON JOHNSON claimed the North Vietnamese attacked a U.S. destroyer & soldiers killed civilians

I remember spies in 1956–1971, when COINTELPRO assaulted a democracy & in the name of protection stalked MARTIN LUTHER KING & comrades

I remember hypocrisy in 1996, when the U.S. government forcefully condemned CASTRO's Committees for the Defense of the Revolution in the U.S. Cuban Liberty and Democratic Solidarity Act...only to implement, 6 years later, JOHN ASHCROFT's strikingly similar operation TIPS

they wanted Cuba to legalize political activity. they wanted Cuba to release political prisoners. they wanted Cuba to commit to fair elections. they wanted Cuba to dissolve

so many game shows, so little time

talking to the teletubbies. again, again :: public broadcasting. we rise: our freedom, our response. responsibility.

DONALD RUMSFELD. you prepare to cremate U.S. soldiers at home, rather than keeping them here in the first place. *it is that simple.* what kind of leverage do we allow you to imagine?

unleashing   waiting   chemicals or be invaded

I remember horror in 1991, when U.S. soldiers such as Timothy McVeigh were ordered to bulldoze Iraqi soldiers & bury them alive, behind the gears of "earth movers"

I remember horror in 1995, when Timothy McVeigh bombed the Murrah Federal Building in protest against the U.S. government, killing 168 people and destroying their families, in one single act

it is that simple.

I remember wrongful captivity from 1942–1949, when the U.S. jailed 110,000 Japanese Americans

it is about oil.

& water.

VANDANA SHIVA: we salute *you.*

2003: journalists asked 1,200 U.S. citizens how many Iraqis were among the 9/11 hijackers & only 17% answered correctly: ZERO. whose war? media war. money war. not our war.

AXIS   OF   EVIL

2003: 1/3 of U.S. citizens polled believed that Weapons of Mass Destruction were found in Iraq and used in this year's war

I wonder how many of us realize that ours is the only country to have ever actually used WMD

democracy is a contact sport

in a constitution far, far away…citizens led public lives & government was transparent. navy suits transpose & stitch impenetrable authority.

the story broke

DENNIS HASTERT, you speak red-handed. diminish people's privacy. diminish public service accountability. diminish corporate accountability. demolish fundamental rights. diminish the fundament. under pretext under pretense you target our neighbors, our immigrants, stripping them violently — whip / lash. no checks. no balance. cooking the books to a crisp.

we can not, we will not, voluntarily, give them up.

living in public is a full-time job.

people disappear for months & return

breathing but the dubyadubyadubya.coma show arrests. he said in his address dramatically, if we contest that SADDAM HUSSEIN is unequivocally evil, "then the word evil has no meaning." yes! go with that! democracy? not happening on my TV. you don't get our words. whose words? our words.

the desperate, to separate: I am not like Bush and point to diction, resort to mockery: "nucular" "Murrka." while regionalisms are normally & ardently granted their space.

but this frustration. this cutting down contagion & reduction. to ugliness.

+

lament a lack of community: do you want one? the little blogs and zines sock on. the proposal & a link to not supremely fucked. MUMIA says, the G8 needs to meet the G8billion. & here you have it. don't move to Paris.

but I do think it's a degree of cockiness and recklessness that we share. which is not a vote in our favor. but leverage. but. I still can't read. I mean: get the forums off the ground.

making less sense than my Swedish grandmother in her late 90s. except: you are bright. except — thank you.

no, here's what I'd do

so what do you need, you need
(1) why we should be against this administration
(2) why we must avert this war
(3) how we can get this admin out (find constitutional lawyers)
(4) how we would replace this admin (perhaps we can ask NELSON MANDELA
     to babysit us while we work out the kinks)
(5) historic revolutions (ties closely to (4))

functional navigation: categories, tiles, & subcats: they have stolen from you,
they are guilty of numerous inhumane acts, they are homeland security's
worst enemy. wretched ENRON.

let the record show that GEORGE H. W. BUSH and the bin Laden family are
many times linked through the CARLYLE GROUP. let the record show that the
bin Ladens have invested upwards of $10 million in a private fund managed
by a former subsidiary of the BECHTEL CORPORATION.

conspiracy *theorists* are out of a job.

yet there is a lot of work to do. hand over the mood-swinging & mind-
changing. weak points in the complex. detectable loads in one of the tests.
we vacillate, they don't. detectably.

"historically" & in the world

stucco-pricked & pierced tomatoes

February 2003: poet Heriberto Yepez reports that U.S. flag-burning has become commonplace in Mexico.

I put the first Vienna Vegetable Orchestra into heavy rotation: sing zucchini! sing squash! sing radish! race the pulse & giggle with glee. otherwise

we are all terrorists

they're pushing legislation that says WE ARE ALL TERRORISTS. at Ashcroft's sole discretion we can be tagged as foreign powers. "any person who engages in clandestine intelligence": your language is slippery, Attorney General. ours is not. we are not, collectively, foreign. but in comparison to thugs we are indeed: clandestine, intelligence.

I remember genocide in 1969 when HENRY KISSINGER led the campaign to bomb Cambodia and Laos, killing one million civilians in the two countries

I remember racial profiling as SEVIS preys upon our brightest students — the blank frames, negatives exposed & discarded

I remember disenfranchisement in 2000 when 8,000 people were falsely called criminals & 57,000 were denied their right to vote by misinformation orchestrated by CHOICEPOINT

& violations of international law in 2003 when CHOICEPOINT sold the date and place of birth, gender, physical description, marital status, passport number, and registered professions of Colombian citizens to the U.S. government for 10 million dollars

occupied even before we arrive. the age of preemptive strikes. law out the window: where are they now? we break glass & go sick the emergencies.

freedom of information act exiled in the name of "terrorism," undefined. world in a safe. tucked away in GUANTANAMO BAY. fed through a crack in the door.

on DELTA AIR I am a credit report. a banking history. a criminal background. a colored tag.

+

FBI agents were deterred from looking into ABDULLAH and OMAR BIN LADEN until 9/13. long long gone. see case ID — 199-EYE WF 213 589.

who else is hiding in cabinets? MULLAH OMAR? TAHA YASSINE RAMADAN? NAJI SABRI? UDAY HUSSEIN? SADDAM HUSSEIN? USAMA BIN LADEN?

lives are blasted apart in missions to capture an endless list of at-large threats to "peace" & they think that commercial breaks can distract our pursuits — of U.S. pursuits.

occupation swept under lying sleeping fat dogs lying. plain clothes anglo big men wielding bigger guns. 97 Iraqi soldiers killed in June 2003. well after the U.S. supposedly won the war. remnants of a Saddam. for whatever it's called: authority. persists in propaganda. AL QA'IDA propped up to us: as an awesome demon.

+

the sergeants & the captains know that something has gone wrong.

cracking barrels

I was this morning thinking hard.

last night I was listening to a CHOMSKY speech in which he cites RONALD REAGAN's failure to acknowledge the international court's indictment of the United States for its illegal acts of war in NICARAGUA. a frightening precedent, since the GEORGE W. BUSH admin seems to be the REAGAN admin on crack. or, more accurately, they are the REAGAN administration on more millions of dollars & accelerated greed.

        LEE RAYMOND

this needs to be said, a lot & again.

        RAY IRANI

this — "representative" "democracy" —
just
ain't
working

flash card. fever down.

"arepa!" as an expletive — translation = pancake. flip flop happy feet: corn is what we've got & worth it.

scholars, watchdogs, tactics, public. thanks to you, CHARLES LEWIS. how long before my membership to anti-slavery international tags me as an accessory to a terrorist organization? naming corporations who use bonded labor to suck oil is, as they say, unpatriotic. read between the pipelines.

if you're free & in. if you're running late. if you're burning a mix. if you're better & better. love. love. wondering. warmth.

the gift of an eye for horror. have tape, will capture. sweetest v-day of the freedom freaks. we shall overthrow. frozen toes or no.

4 million in the streets & all mobile, save NYC. saying no to war were college students, middle-aged couples, families, veterans of the 60s civil rights movement, Average White Guys for Peace, laborers, environmentalists, Christians, businessfolk, and elderly ladies wearing pink kerchiefs who, after 80 years of globalization, just — can't — take it anymore!

rage & helplessness abound within barricades, controlled, inward, still denied assembly. right to sidewalks kicked to the curb. beating the penned-in kneeling puppets, chickens watch. standoff in SoHo rings DROP BUSH, NOT BOMBS!

+

their F-15 = detect / acquire / track / attack. the single-seat, low-drag, superior-weapon, Eagle air.

mythological in stature: war reasons & their means.

actual in cost: $2,000 per family, here; entire families, there.

M27 (g00d girl)

I am so deeply ashamed to be at work today.

the occupation is estimated at 800 billion dollars. public schools. die in.

an American socialist weighs in, & as long. a criminal soul. prison & tradition. ice cap asks to be born. isn't. old. motto stage, quotation state, "can't... anybody play?"

>   LOWRY MAYS

slavery still going on. and we have to worry about slanderous lawsuits in naming the aggressors. CHARLES R. WILLIAMSON. bone meal or warhead. "please, sir, may I have another." dichotomy.

the die-in I skipped.

>   KARL ROVE

for webconnect. what is radically new.

>   SANFORD WEILL

upper-upper echelon action enriches their own / private / pirate / booty. be damned!, we form. in human. pacifist bands. us together. G8billion. a stunning

>   LINES_OF_YELLING
>   LINES_OF_YELLING_2
>   LINES_OF_YELLING_3

introducing

every Italian grandmother looks like mine

when the women at my voting poll in Brooklyn rant about my green
registration I know they blame me for Bush's stolen office. "but," I want to
say, "AL GORE is an OCCIDENTAL shareholder!" still I feel ashamed to upset
them like this. I want to apologize. & maybe get a hug.

one of them says, "I'd be curious to know *why* —" but I feel too afraid to
indulge the invitation.

I see my own grandmother wrapped sweet in an afghan. her name was
REPETTO. she married a potato-famine exile. I never knew: her first fiancé,
her real eyebrows.

everything I feel is wrong

the blood of 1.2 million Iraqis in the last 12 years is on our hands. I know & I know, daily. emotional paralysis not productive but this is not a spot to out.

invoking the mantra: "to make a world worth saving"

I appreciate our cosmic balance: when I'm up, you're down — when you're down, I'm up. what keeps us here. I want to marry: definitive juxtapositions. I desperately need: tons of work.

'easy action' concept: full-throttle on the portal. grassroots people, friends directly.

cherry notes to the agriculture. please-to-be prepared for me. or don't. but as for getting in the same room: playing out the /rupture threads. I would just like a promise on even, the horizon. she / death / casually / real.

the future is now. reggae when you need her. the PATRIOT ACT II is 120 pages long with endless reams of references, rendering it purposely unreadable. laborious task after work — but that's what we're looking at: 13,000 Muslims under threat of deportation.

the magic of my sisters & this morning

being with those family people, feeling love & feeling happy, taking care: of every one.

to draw a line down humankind: I'd dare you but you'd hate yourself in the interminable mourning. pick truth not dare. s'il vous plaît. that is not a question & that is: not a question. have complex reactions, we will I promise catch them.

this story within a tenement building: I love / under construction. los amigos invisibles. concede that being forced endurance, can be helpful.

comrades. I don't imagine there is any way to avert a renewed war. I must imagine we can & will avert a renewed war. on the Iraqi people.

bhangra to the gold teeth thief. brain depart too cloudy to communicate. I feel a ghost in here / I feel a god in here.

I feel a guard in here.

or a little continuity. at this point, they're starving. diverting water to dilute our anniversaries. plane overhead. flash. up. gasp.

falling more on the alkaline side, a danger in lethargic — lifestyle, living. stressing our already sunken depression. greens in balance — militant? unthinkable. who houses the hidden egos. on all sides. crowded to me. hope for space. outer, not ordered.

meaning you'd be safe. but that's not what they said. scientists confused.

CONDOLEEZZA RICE

I may be crashing into pound puppy love, weakened by our close blood ties & resigning expectations, occupation. but I'd really like to go.

CPR to our blackened memory. what else. I am vital media probing reticent carvings. space collective, when a corporation was called a company. author's names in the live show erased.

GEORGE SCHULTZ

I am a lucky human & continue & astonished. I'm glad you need me. I found him in documents. & all this trouble. he stopped drinking milk. & I'm obsessed with milk, now. complicated swimming.

clearly he's bored & I have no patience. Matt was crying in a heavy iron pot. the pot wasn't hurt. that day or so of stasis.

I look for new articles. I do a bad job. "she" is not a doctor. nothing is before.

luck with the day & concerned about blood about potential organ damage. reversing it. further. I post a peace message: this global city is smaller than we often like to believe. free to be: willfully ignorant. in theory I'm upfront. but but this this dumb awkward fear of conversation among ourselves. the unbearable lightness of being American.

NEW ORDER

blue monday

truth comes out like a stain. praise woman in her disappearing, in this long wrecked juncture, this profane ear-heart.

the boy died because

filthy shelf-life keeps us from the files.

& everything that chooses you

((i want the word 'agile' [here]))

would cool off, the dull knife twists

+

a screened-in porch. cocktail collapse against a sheer wall & rearing. loses. sleep: the fake sober. schoolgirl. smoking. portland. memory.

rain is shining so we can flee. & karma. & by some force. it's quiet. & there are stairs & you're on the stars & i am crying. happy like a sake bouquet. i do this early in the valentine.

+

transatlantic no man lands. organ trials kick the dark, & stardead court. i would have explained —

an atmosphere on dignity charming their poisons. the patent illogic on top. flesh & skin absurdly left out. in rain to shine the system.

substance

but i can make tonight another day

match killer, budget problems, closing time on greed-plump tyranny.

welfare kitty sings a last meow before their bloodshot eyes. hot summer nest-egg, hatches to die on the job. vicious cycle pedals transparent: balance sheets of iron fists. committing to capital, outlook panicked & multiplied performance, erroneously so. it's a case of existing, and not-thinking. "junk" — "science" — all over / the horizon.

gun owner, gun grabber, let alone participate. gray apparent & slaps in the face. academic nannies filling potholes. u.s. populace spending 17 billion dollars a year on books & 105 billion dollars on booze.

& yet i write we write. american women married. naturally k street standing behind. numbers & o cannabis.

petitions exceed force as usual. reduce formal logic & the error-checked agenda. flunked a urinalysis. malpractice mapped & theocratic.

wheel was riskier. chimpanzee cancer. tax-dollar screening. i am a monster.

+

living ads up in a usa chromosome. the unspoken tortures that western life demands. nikes on sale. computer home peripherals. incidental compounds. chests of costume jewelry. landfill, leadership.

i can contribute & bemoan. my options dotted lines. they call it "cell damage," or learning as i go.

my friend & i thought that working with designer clothes meant we would be clear of sweatshops. silly us. stupid us & dumb we are. made with pride.

minddose: a right direction. blood shortage the abyss, prior to use, weeks cover gas tanks fit for an army. soccer. practice. comfort.

net gains & insider trading, later that morning, or "news," announcing:

low life

head over fist. not dead yet.

ruffled collars writhe in manifestos. egregious gesture, to say grace.

stringed monopoly concerts gore & the neverending sting. liberal douse of gasoline on raging oppositions: for immigrants (let them in), to your hearts: how precisely.

the goodbook says — guttered kitten brown teeth. she's no longer boldly. off the resist & counting wheels. as they wheel by. cobblestone imprints smell / the / tradition. fate might be a controlative saltmine, a smack queen special.

segregationist. old campaign in a new real estate. an armageddon atrium.

no more mr. archive. rising backdrop & since unsealed, epiphany at all those brazilian voters. but all this action couldn't squelch a make-out fantasy (kiss — kiss —)

an unplugged time to jack in — willfully, recklessly, criminally, spastically, breaking — bread.

as for the suit: to overlap hunger.

+

to the classical ethicist: your scenarios never happen in real life (there is no "minus" in "class"). a violin prodigy needing a transplant and 4 "regular" people — so what if they are also ill & likely — never happen in a real room, in the same time. it's called strata.

he who gets to choose among them also gets to make up their lives. & their deaths. utilitarian in a global economy.   utopic in a euphemism. willful / stranger / in a strangled land.

a simple annexation.

denial

long-winded change :: conceit of moral mudflaps

evangelical reckonings spark angels to counteract the bad ballot system. they have expressed a lot of fear.

choice point. would be the point. velvet rope revolution. lemon revival & ribbons on trees. nevada brothel: contact me catholic. already alienated, meaty crop of bishops.

if your culture is broke :: extrapolate

they don't like us at all & fierce games will follow. killings part of the unaccountable contract. customary blow to us stupid layfolk. pork to pyrotechnics to pulp lies blushing. hidden: pray-ers.

pruning the spoiled 'happy day' thesis. appear to be irrational. or else indifferent. group delusions: drop weight, exacerbate.

aftermath a natural stage. nearly locked: into a chronic

+

i want to deal directly. consciousness the other, true heritage & our tragedies. would be avoided if sincere in their gasp. way too tight on certain segments of the population: cf southeast, in some so-called home, in the district of columbia.

let's make a deal: policy the militarism & live to our words. cause you're lying & you're lying & you're lying. & you need to stop lying. or else. keep out. no girls will refrain from trying you for treason.

one-third of usamerican children born today will develop diabetes by adult-hood. food that is actually food. not mutually exclusive.

own fear. deep dish. piggish falsehood destroys ecology & i can detect. tremendous dysfunction. charging the tv. parent to dramas. phantoms pass & default the conclusions — all in the foreground

of anywhere but here. cul-de-sac attack. take some shelter & FREEDOM FRIES the drive-thru
home.

reason versus justification. masquerade a habitat. welcome to caution & to our native language. diluted daily. over 6 billion served.

he puts his foot in my teeth.

generation nation brought up by design. you can't talk and listen — at the same time. you can't produce and think — at the same time. you can't consume and conserve — at the same time. preserving. our breathing. a real punch in the kidneys.

three cheers for our relatives: a bunch of raving lunatics. muscle the mouth & trigger the itch. they're smarter than your average sling.

shot.

so i'm sitting here.

so hit me.

dreams never die

all left what loathe. lost explosions & the way children. shed. the rebirth.

pipe dreams goliath pundits — power failure — lights out. candles we might skewer the noonday go-it-alone leatherneck.

fictions. striking. tide. over.

coming in your coil by straddling this war. or any war. little bird gift wakes exuberant   marriage   from   paranoia

bad time between them

meeting under maple, we all start :: two simple cells. expired from political reality, hype rage: that state can feed. running man, the mr. freeze, please daze the predator & pre-date the sick day // almost there.

major breath of culture workers, charlatans sincere. breeding mark fades evenly to sand yet she can still sense it granular. everywhere & fringe to match.

pixie dust i miss you compassion

me too one night i met a boy

& now i'm going there

i'm absorbed into porousness. you haunt the past into behaving. future too. present perfect. back to bed.

the two of swords, or what makes us madness. nagging at my back there is a dull and constant memory of a six-year-old. with spinal injuries. baghdad — april — "spring" & all

+

tossing about the heavy blink i blanket you to make it stop. i give you a bath & some relief. while outside a liar. ghost me i'm cold

attempting market & serving kale, i'd steam our temples open too. firmly in for hydrated company. better / head / quarters, get your meal cards due in writing. in nonetheless longevity.

+

how she is that sandman & generic. blocking the razing of a dreamlife because there are a lot of people. sir. drinking wine in gardens. babylon origins. coincidental elephants.

smashfrog thunderclap. cut it out & call me.

i mean i thought i was blind.

courtyard worship, limestone trouble / with mortals in their naked, or their naked

i'm not bleeding. i'm not human.

+

parting from the underlake & a little weak. trouble with gods. brotherhood fraught. my impermanent delight, or your illusive wonder — a turtle for the crawling. magic shell or toxic shell. old lace or lead based.

i can pretend i can pretend & fireflies a world a flicker

beaten moon vernacular wrappings — hands up & exit slowly. addict sounds the door in love. how many poems called dreams? the long walk, the waking life.

spirit of the night light hangs another step. the drinking glass is not a lie. have a seat inside a letter. trembling erect does no one good but afraid & a ration — of power will or walls.

for every potential to be played out — what planetary green we'd need. trade abuse for endurance. answers for infinity. personae for a person. truth is an expression. & impressive: between.

you'll never make without love. done really. belly fortune. capture after. master vary oil from the sun / down / flower / petal

+

when i started living urgently. cyclically, as the core of a lettuce head looked like babies from a good soil. good for them. fractals & imperfections protecting us from psychic death.

i am a psychic fascist. or confess to latch to content if it's clearly altruistic. i can believe / i have no needs.

lettuce bright & sweet   like   strawberry, like b.c.

+

carcrash perspective tailgates our wake, just when the tailgating trend had safely seemed passé. novel junky constantly fleeting in paradox & in hypodermics. & in worry, all our worry. hope into remission.

dialects possess by the five-sensed person, or the caustic or imprisoned. for good. the lover. the hater. the banker the jeweler the diva the gardener. we'll like that gardener. he is already — outside. working, not waiting. making, not labor.

the debate, as if it's blame. we are not all such kindred spirits & as such are ok. clock such as ok.

(the car question abstract is frightening. if we lie down with beings who look like us because they are familiar — because we spend our time with family, and look-a-likes are therefore safe — then what are we doing with big metal mobiles? look who's coming to dinner. lounging with a caddy.)

hooked on commercials, a horrific —   compilation. needle / haystack / stitching / surgery. it means actually. truth this time.

+

realized consumed. fall in the eyes of the gps cattle. flawed servitude, or of a different kind. as in send them the ransom, & set the captives loose. ego desires go unending

why not aim, what is life: in this world, if not you

invisible — fence

decorate in mermaids

decorated soundminds

rapidly exceeding

supposed ends & sunspots

the dizzying compress

truly i love

a view to the closer

strength not power

+

proof

there is no

fundamental difference:

everybody looks the same

in here these bloody clothes

REFERENCES

199-EYE-WF 213 589: Document uncovered by journalist Greg Palast, who explains that 199 means national security, and WF means that Washington field office special agents were conducting the investigation; the subjects of the investigation were Abdullah bin Laden and the World Assembly of Muslim Youth (WAMY), a suspected terrorist organization (*BBC*, 6 Nov 2001)

MUMIA ABU-JAMAL: Award-winning journalist known for exposing police violence against communities of color; on death row since 1982 for his alleged shooting of a police officer; many maintain that he has been denied a fair trial (www.amnesty.org; *New York Newsday*, 1995)

AFGHANISTAN: Site of Usama bin Laden following the 9/11/2001 attacks on the U.S.; site of Taliban regime; site of 10/7/2001 attack by the U.S., which promised yet-to-be-realized reconstruction under martial law

AL QA'IDA: Translates to "base force"; multinational organization, established in 1991 to unite Muslims and establish a Caliphate government

JOHN ASHCROFT: U.S. attorney general; architect of the Patriot Act II, which diminishes constitutional rights and privacy of public citizens, residents, and visitors; act empowers attorney general as the sole judge of suspicious activity, in vaguely defined situations (www.public-i.org)

AXIS OF EVIL: Term coined in G.W. Bush's January 2002 State of the Union address to include Iran, Iraq, and North Korea, identifying them as being governed by opaque, repressive regimes; later expanded to include Syria, Libya, and Cuba

JAMES A. BAKER III: Senior counselor, The Carlyle Group, which buys and controls oil, arms, and state leaders (www.alternet.org, 4 Mar 2003)

BECHTEL CORPORATION: Private engineering-construction corporation that won a contract to rebuild Iraq, worth $68 million in the short run, up to $680 million in the long run (www.usaid.org); did business with Saddam when he was known to be committing crimes of humanity against Iranians and Iraqis; was former parent of the Fremont Group, which operates a private equity fund that received a $10 million investment from the bin Laden family prior to 9/11 (cooperativeresearch.org/corporation/profiles/bechtel.html)

ABDULLAH BIN LADEN: Brother of Usama; would-be target of investigation 199-EYE WF 213 589

OMAR BIN LADEN: Brother of Usama; would-be target of investigation 199-EYE WF 213 589

USAMA BIN LADEN: Self-proclaimed mastermind of 9/11 attacks on U.S.; among the U.S. 10 Most Wanted (www.emergency.com, 21 Feb 2003)

GEORGE H.W. BUSH: Former U.S. president (1988–92); former U.S. vice president (1980–88); former CIA director; led the Gulf War (Oil War I) initiative; founder of Zapata Petroleum; current board member of the Carlyle Group

GEORGE W. BUSH: President of the United States, whose office was established by specious means (*The Nation*, 5 Feb 2001); executed 152 people during his tenure as governor of Texas

CARLYLE GROUP: $12 billion private equity group; manages financial assets of the Saudi Binladen Corp (SBC), headed by the bin Laden family, who were key to G.W. Bush's acquisition of petroleum concessions (millions of dollars) from Bahrain when he led the Harken Energy Corp (www.globalresearch.ca, 1 Oct 2001); Charles Lewis points out that Carlyle Group connections between the Bush and bin Laden families mean that "George W. Bush could, some day, benefit financially from his own administration's decisions, through his father's investments"

FIDEL CASTRO: Cuba's prime minister, 1959–76, head of state, 1976–present; developed confrontational relationship with the U.S. following the 1961 Bay of Pigs invasion and the 1962 Cuban Missile Crisis; Castro's regime is a known enemy to human rights and Cuba is widely regarded as a police state (usinfo.state.gov)

NICHOLAS D. CHABRAJA: Chairman and CEO, General Dynamics, which manufactures F-16 jets, Abrams tanks, and Trident subs; holds contracts in the billions with the U.S. government (contracts.corporate.findlaw.com)

DICK CHENEY: Ex-CEO, Halliburton, a role in which he earned the corporation millions in Iraq; vice president of the U.S. (*San Francisco Bay Guardian*, 13 Nov 2000)

CHOICEPOINT: Parent company of DataBase Technologies, hired by Florida's Governor Jeb Bush and Secretary of State Katherine Harris to filter felons and suspected felons, as well as people whose names and birth dates happen to match either group, from Florida's pool of voters; consequently, 57,000 people were barred from voting without due process, 90% of whom were Democrats, the majority black; ChoicePoint's board consists of Republican-party investors and lobbyists (www.democracynow.org, 7 May 2003; www.alternet.org, 17 Mar 2003; *Washington Monthly*, 26 Aug 2002)

NOAM CHOMSKY: Professor of linguistics, M.I.T.; renowned intellectual, author, activist, and civil libertarian

VANCE D. COFFMAN: Chairman and CEO, Lockheed Martin, world's top military contractor, maker of the U-2, SR-71, F-16, F/A-22, and javelin missiles

COINTELPRO: FBI counterintelligence program established in 1956 that incorporated fraud and force to sabotage legally protected political activity; declared unconstitutional in 1971

PHILIP M. CONDIT: Former chairman and CEO, Boeing, maker of "smart" bombs, F-15 fighters, and Apache helicopters

DELTA AIR: Corporate airline that partnered with U.S. intelligence following 9/11 to run CAPPS II (Computer Assisted Passenger Prescreening System), acquiring confidential information about its customers and tagging them with red, yellow, and green threat-levels (*The New York Times*, 6 Mar 2003)

ENRON: Energy corporation that reported fraudulent earnings by recording revenue as the total value of its traded goods, without deducting its costs, ending in its filing for bankruptcy and subsequently financially devastating thousands of employees and shareholders (*BBC*, 22 Aug 2002; www.corpwatch.org, 20 Jul 2000); poured hundreds of thousands of dollars into G.W. Bush's campaigns (*Guardian Unlimited*, 24 Jan 2002); Enron execs visited the White House six times in 2001 to help the administration plan its energy policy (*Los Angeles Times*, 26 Aug 2001); in 2000, Enron CEO Kenneth Lay and his wife Linda spent $4 million on variable annuities that will in 2007 guarantee them an annual income of $900,000 for life (*Mother Jones*, 21 Feb 2002)

F15: February 15, 2003, an international day of protest in which an estimated 4 million people around the world took to the streets in opposition to the U.S.- and UK-led renewed war on the Iraqi people; largest protest in recorded history (*CNN*, 15 Feb 2003)

FCC: U.S. Federal Communications Committee, directed by Michael Powell, son of Colin Powell (U.S. secretary of state who owned $13.3 million in AOL stock before its merger with Time Warner — a merger approved by a committee of 5, including son Michael); moved to deregulate media ownership in 2003 so that a single company could own a newspaper and a television station in the same market, diminishing community-oriented programming (*NOW with Bill Moyers*, 25 Oct 2002)

FREEDOM FRIES: Phrase to replace "french fries," used by some in the U.S. to express their disdain for France, in its government's opposition to the proposed war on Iraq

AMY GOODMAN: Journalist, hosts the daily radio show *Democracy Now!*; tireless champion for peace and justice

AL GORE: Former vice president of the U.S.; supported sanctions against Iraq throughout his 8-year term, which, among other factors, compelled many social-democrat voters to support third-party candidates in the 2000 presidential election

GUANTANAMO BAY: U.S. naval base in Cuba; site of detention camp that holds masses of immigrants under specious charges; notorious for its brutal conditions; on April 23, 2003, the U.S. military admitted that children younger than 16 were being held as "enemy combatants," which human-rights groups condemn as illegal (*The New York Times*, 16 Sep 2002)

DENNIS HASTERT: Speaker of the U.S. House of Representatives, signed a draft of the Patriot Act II prior to denying any knowledge of the proposed Act (*NOW with Bill Moyers*, 7 Feb 2003)

SADDAM HUSSEIN: Dictator of Iraq, 1979–2003; guilty of numerous, brutal crimes against Iranians and Iraqis; sought and captured by U.S. government

UDAY HUSSEIN: Elder son of Saddam; notorious murderer and torturer (*Associated Press*, 23 Jul 2003); killed by U.S. troops (*CNN*, 22 Jul 2003)

RAY IRANI: Chairman and CEO, Occidental Petroleum

IRAQ: Invaded Kuwait in 1990, leading to UN sanctions against the nation, resulting in 1.2 million Iraqi deaths from 1991–2003; site of U.S.-led invasion "Operation Desert Storm" in 1991; site of U.S.- and UK-led "Operation Infinite Liberty" (OIL) in 2003, renamed "Operation Infinite Justice," the end of which was declared by G.W. Bush on May 1, but fighting continues under U.S.- and UK-led occupation (www.mideastweb.org/iraqtimeline.htm)

LYNDON JOHNSON: Former U.S. president; launched the War on Poverty and supported civil rights in the U.S.; escalated U.S. engagement in Vietnam War

HAMID KARZAI: Afghan head of state; noted anti-Soviet combatant; maintains amiable rapport with U.S. (*BBC*, 14 Jun 2002)

KHAD: Afghanistan branch of KGB; assassinated Meena (see below)

MARTIN LUTHER KING, JR.: Revered leader of the U.S. Civil Rights movement; assassinated in 1968

HENRY KISSINGER: Former U.S. secretary of state, wanted for war crimes and human rights abuses in Vietnam, Cambodia, Laos, Indonesia, Cyprus, Kurdistan, Bangladesh, East Timor, and Chile, where Kissinger helped to plan the 9/11/1973 overthrow of the democratically elected President Salvador Allende (Christopher Hitchens, *The Trial of Henry Kissinger*)

CHARLES LEWIS: Executive director of the nonprofit, nonpartisan Center for Public Integrity, which first brought the Patriot Act II to the public's attention; said "democracy is a contact sport" (www.public-i.org)

M27: March 27, 2003, die-in at Rockefeller Center, NYC, protesting the war in Iraq; 170 people arrested (WBAI, 27 Mar 2003)

NELSON MANDELA: President of South Africa, 1994–1999; unjustly imprisoned under Apartheid rule from 1962 to 1990

AHMAD SHAH MASSOUD: Leader of the Northern Alliance (U.S. ally) until his assassination on 9/9/2001, which is believed to be related to the 9/11 plan of attack on the U.S. (*Christian Science Monitor*, 20 Feb 2002)

LOWRY MAYS: Chairman and CEO, Clear Channel, which programs 1,200 U.S. radio stations, transmitting pro-war content and censoring voices of dissent (e.g., in its ban of the anti-war country musicians The Dixie Chicks)

MEENA: Martyred, founding leader of the Revolutionary Association of the Women of Afghanistan (RAWA)

K. RUPERT MURDOCH: Chairman and CEO, News Corporation Ltd; owns Fox News, which is notorious for shock-jock programming, where reports are sensationalized in order to manipulate viewers' emotional responses to news content

NICARAGUA: Site of 1984 U.S. sabotage, in which the CIA was discovered to have laid land mines to destroy Sandinista operations; the U.S. Senate condemned the minings, 84–12; the Sandinistas took the case to the International Court of Justice (aka the World Court) and won, but the Reagan administration refused to acknowledge the court's jurisdiction (International Court of Justice, 27 June 1986)

NORTH KOREA: Self-proclaimed manufacturer and harborer of nuclear weapons, which is not under U.S. attack, and, to note, does not sit on top of oil; claims it is breaking its end of the Geneva agreement by resuming production of nuclear weapons because the U.S. violated its end of the agreement, which was to complete the construction of light water reactors by the end of 2003 (*BBC*, 9 Jun 2003)

OCCIDENTAL PETROLEUM: Energy corporation whose operations in Colombia are protected by U.S. military aid; supports armed groups and human rights violators; achieved notoriety in the 1990s with its threat to forcibly remove the U'wa tribe from their sacred land in order to lay an oil pipeline (www.amazonwatch.org, 14 Aug 2000; *Colombia Now!*, May 2003)

MULLAH OMAR: Taliban leader, sought by the U.S. government; states that "greater good" is destroying America (*BBC*, 15 Nov 2001)

PATRIOT ACT II: Formally known as the Domestic Security Enhancement Act of 2003: the ACLU says that this act, under the pretext of fighting terrorism, diminishes personal privacy by removing checks on government power; diminishes public accountability by increasing government secrecy; diminishes corporate accountability; undermines fundamental constitutional rights of Americans under overbroad definitions of "terrorism" and "terrorist organization"; and unfairly targets immigrants

SALAM PAX: Baghdad resident whose weblog "Where Is Raed?" is a key source of news for an international readership (dearraed.blogspot.com)

AUGUSTO PINOCHET: Dictator of Chile from 1973 to 1990, having taken power following the U.S.-sponsored coup d'état of democratically elected President Salvador Allende; presided over the murder and disappearance of more than 3,000 Chilean citizens (*BBC*, 27 Sep 1999)

TAHA YASSINE RAMADAN: Vice president of Iraq under Saddam Hussein; notorious for his numerous crimes against humanity (*BBC*, 16 Oct 2002); detained by U.S. government (www.arabicnews.com, 20 Aug 2003)

LEE RAYMOND: Chairman and CEO, ExxonMobil, the world's largest energy corporation and the largest contributor to G.W. Bush's campaign; responsible for oil spills, human rights abuses, and tax evasions (*BBC*, 22 Jun 2001; *Associated Press*, 10 Sep 2003)

RONALD REAGAN: Former U.S. president whose term included the Iran-Contra scandal and, consequently, 30 administration members in prison

JEANETTE REPETTO: My grandmother, who shaved her eyebrows and changed her name in order to disguise her ethnicity and get a job in 1920s NYC

CONDOLEEZZA RICE: U.S. national security advisor; former director of the board at ChevronTexaco

KARL ROVE: Strategist for G.W. Bush; known as "Bush's brain"; believed to have been the architect of the U.S.- and UK-renewed war on Iraq to improve Bush's political prospects (*BuzzFlash*, 5 June 2003)

ARUNDHATI ROY: Internationally celebrated author, speaker, and activist for peace and justice

DONALD RUMSFELD: U.S. secretary of defense; ensured that military would employ the B-1 bomber, Trident Sub, and MX Missile; served as Nixon advisor from 1970 to 1973 (*PBS NewsHour*, 28 Dec 2000)

NAJI SABRI: Foreign minister of Iraq under Saddam Hussein; sought by U.S. government

GEORGE SCHULTZ: Senior counselor, Bechtel Corporation, which dumps nuclear waste and hijacks Bolivia's water (news.pacificnews.org, 8 Nov 2002)

SEVIS: Student Exchange and Visitor Information System, which releases private information about all U.S. inhabitants who are not citizens; all schools and organizations welcoming such persons have been required to pursue re-certification under this program (www.stopsevis.org)

VANDANA SHIVA: Ph.D. physicist, author, and activist against water privatization, gender discrimination, biotechnology and genetic engineering, and ecological destruction

RONALD SUGAR: CEO and president, Northrop Grumman, manufacturer of B2 stealth bomber

TIPS: Terrorist Information and Prevention System, designed by John Ashcroft to recruit citizens to report to the U.S. government their neighbors' suspected terrorist-related activity (www.aclu.org)

UNOCAL: Energy corporation that in 1997 presented the Taliban with a contract for nearly $4 billion to allow the construction of an oil pipeline across Afghanistan (*WorldPress*, 18 Oct 2001; www.worldpress.org/specials/pp/pipeline_timeline.htm)

VENEZUELA: Site of 24-hour, U.S.-led coup d'état of democratically elected President Hugo Chavez, which was overturned by a massive citizen demand for the return and reinstatement of Chavez; under Chavez, OPEC has been revitalized, and oil from Venezuela to the U.S. is now priced at 2 to 3 times more than it had been when Venezuela was ruled by the right-wing party COPEI (*NOW with Bill Moyers*, 19 Apr 2002; http://www.narconews.com/alphandary2.html)

SANFORD WEILL: Chairman and CEO, Citigroup, which funds oil pipelines, predatory loans, deforestation, and prison construction (*Multinational Monitor*, Apr 2002)

PAUL WELLSTONE: Democratic senator from Minnesota who died in a plane crash in October 2002; ardently outspoken against a proposed attack on Iraq; many believe his death to have been a murder, executed by the U.S. government forces he opposed (www.alternet.org, 28 Oct 2002; www.investigate911.com/wellstonemurder.htm)

CHARLES R. WILLIAMSON: Chairman and CEO, Unocal Corp, which maintains amiable rapport with regimes in Burma, Indonesia, and Afghanistan (*Los Angeles Times*, 2 Jun 1998)

PAUL WOLFOWITZ: Deputy secretary of defense; formerly served on the board of Northrop Grumman, a leading weapons manufacturer

A C K N O W L E D G M E N T S

Creation is communal.

I am grateful to many friends and communities for their support in researching and producing this book: Jules Boykoff; the Circulars community; Allison Cobb; Patricia Dienstfrey; Jed Distler and Composers Collaborative; David Daniell; Natasha Dwyer; Laura Elrick; Eric Keenaghan; Tom Orange; David Perry; the Poetry Is News confer-ence; Kristin Prevallet; Matt Raines; *RELAY* subscribers, who forgave my failure to issue newsletters while I pursued this project; Kaia Sand; The Social Mark; Juliana Spahr; Subpoetics; Rodrigo Toscano; and Charles Weigl, who identified "the unbearable lightness of being American."

I am indebted to many writers, journalists, and collectives for investigative reports and essays that provided testimony and provoked considerations regarding situations in Afghanistan and Iraq: *Afghan Communicator*; Michael Albert; *AlterNet*; The American Civil Liberties Union; Paul Anderson; Scott Baldouf; Terry Bisson; Eric Bosse; Nancy Rivera Brooks; Abigail Caplovitz; Michael Cassidy; Pratap Chatterjee; Rich Cowan; FAIR; Robert Fisk; Juan Gonzalez; *The Guardian*; Barnaby Hall; Bill Hogan; *The Inde-pendent*; Mark Karlin; Martin A. Lee; Pamela Mewes; Will Miller; Bill Moyers; Michael I. Niman; Greg Palast; Judy Pasternak; Ted Rall; Paul Rosenberg; Patrick J. Sloyan; The Ruckus Society; Edward Said; Jim Shultz; Nicholas Thompson; Mark Tran; and *ZMag*.

I thank the editors of the publications in which some of these poems first appeared: Kevin Killian and Dodie Bellamy, *Mirage/Periodical #109*; Diane Ward and Phyllis Rosenzweig, *Primary Writing*.

I am especially appreciative for my sisters, Katie Mugnai and Janice Tumulty, for their magnanimous love and support, in which they keep alive the spirits of our parents.

— CM